NIXES MATE REVIEW

ISSUE 32|33 SUMMER|FALL 2024

Nixes Mate Books
Allston, Massachusetts

All works copyrighted by their authors, 2024.

Book design by Michael McInnis.
Cover image used with permission.

All rights reserved. This book or any portion thereof may not be reproduced or used in any manner whatsoever without the express written permission of the publisher except for the use of brief quotations in a book review or scholarly journal.

Jackie Balter · Intern
Philip Borenstein · Publisher Emeritus
Hannah Larrabee · Editor + Explorer
Michael McInnis · Designer + Factotum
Annie Elezabeth Pluto · Editor + Director

ISBN 978-1-949279-58-0

Nixes Mate Publications
POBox 1179
Allston, MA 02134
nixesmate.pub

¡Ghost bicycles, hurricanes, elections, war! No one could have predicted this. Well, they did, but don't let that spoil *your* truth, *our* truth, *a* truth.

Here at Nixes Mate headquarters, graveyard for pirates, mutineers, and booze cruises, we can't sit still. This is our biggest issue and features 29 new authors to *Nixes Mate Review*.

¡Trust us! ¡We've made poetry taste better!

Nixes Mate headquarters at high tide.

Waiting in the Wings · Gerald Yelle | 3

Ignorance · Catherine Fahey | 4

Three Micro Flashes · Humayun Malik | 5

Untended · Susan Tepper | 6

monument maker · Charlotte Friedman | 7

Naming the Animals · Joan Mazza | 9

By the Numbers · Buffy Shutt | 10

The Rabbit Dies · Sara Eddy | 12

Afterlife · Ruth Smullin | 13

Effigy · Laurin Becker Macios | 15

A Gymnast Relives · Eric Braude | 16

Gifts from My Father · Mark Walsh | 17

Why I Am Not Aging · Stephen Kampa | 19

When my husband on our wedding anniversary · Laurel Benjamin | 20

Skinship · Tom Laughlin | 21

Big Sur · Ed Gaudet | 22

So Much Depends · Brian Mosher | 23

Japanese Beetle · Claire McMillan | 24

Cupid's spade · Ruchi Acharya | 25

Making Babies · Zvi A. Sesling | 26

Night Swim · Karen Poppy | 27

At the Lake · Beth Boylan | 30

Ode to Frank O'Hara's Hands · Beth Boylan | 31

list poem · Jack Giaour | 32

Hookus · Robert Carr | 33

It's a Risk to Write About Sex · Robin Dellabough | 34

Nightstand · Adam Grabowski | 35

a/sunder · Sandra Fees | 36

Table of Contents

37 | Where do I go from here? · Elly Guzikowski
38 | Improv Student Showcase · Jon Wesick
40 | Explaining "the patron saint of suicide" · Matthew E. Henry
48 | the patron saint of suicide · Matthew E. Henry
50 | In Summer · Jacqueline Coleman-Fried
52 | Cantata for Chemo Infusion Pack · Neal Silberblatt
53 | This Is Not a Ghazal · Rusty Barnes
54 | Near Edmond, Oklahoma: August · Dale Cottingham
55 | The Year I Went Without Being Discovered · Mark DeCarteret
56 | Little Madam, · Susanna Rich
57 | The Oil Man Tells Me All About the Bobcat in His Yard · Rachel Becker
58 | Sad Maryanne · Brad Rose
59 | Silk · Grace Massey
60 | Curb Appeal But Don't Open the Front Door · Jeffry Bernstein
61 | Horseshoes & Red Wine · John Dorsey
62 | On the Tenth Anniversary of Our Ghosting, · Jennifer Martelli
63 | A Poem With Spoilers · Jennifer Martelli
64 | To Lunge a Horse · Cal Freeman
66 | Landscapes of Silence · Sara Letourneau
68 | Botany · Hannah Larrabee
69 | There Were so Many Fucking Whales · Karina Jutzi
70 | Imagine what tree tells owl · Miriam O'Neal
71 | How to Leave · Michael Quattrone

REVIEWS:

72 | *Marble Dust* | Gary Metras (Červená Barva Press) · Miriam O'Neal
74 | *Jinx and Heavenly Calling* | Kelly DuMar (Lily Poetry Books) · Jackie Balter
76 | Author Biographies

Waiting in the Wings

Gerald Yelle

I heard the flap of a Sunday morning
wingbeat like a heartbeat
and the rustling of a Sunday paper.
It kept time with the squawk
of a jay hawk that sounded like a jay
though it wouldn't let me see it.
It might've known I was waiting
to see if it were hawk or jay and it
must've felt like waiting
for me to stop waiting like we
were both waiting as if waiting had
come into its own like a standing
wave where all there is
is waiting. And waiting is the thing
you wait for. The long wait in
a line that doesn't move. Where
everybody thinks the thing
they've waited for is about to drop.

Ignorance

Catherine Fahey

    Do you like Nine Inch Nails? asks Meaghan, black
    nail polish & red hair, ripped tights, blue ink
    drawings on her knees, you can't see my knees
    under my uniform skirt. She "forgot"
    her vest & her bra strap is showing through
    her blouse, distracting me. I see my own
    hands with dirt & ink & paint & hangnails
    bitten off; nails that long are fully out
    of uniform & I'd get detention;
    punished at home, where once we prayed against
    Madonna's Immaculate Collection;
    but if my father actually listened
    to Trent Reznor he'd find such common ground
    "I'd rather die than give you control" – Dad.

Three Micro Flashes

Humayun Malik

KEY OF LOVE

Sex.

NOT FOR SELL

"Love."

NOT TO PRACTICE

Crime.

Untended

Susan Tepper

I don't have your thick woods
or fires in the grate.
No bushy lilacs to push aside
when I walk into the garden –
mine is tight buildings
without clematis
Fire escapes trailing the brick
hand over hand.
I watched him pass
my window at dawn,
gated –
his sneakers and jeans
bypassing me
for one of sheer glass.
I shivered at the prospect.
Some sleeping woman
who couldn't afford extra
in this city garden.
Wildly overgrown, untended.

monument maker

Charlotte Friedman

Between Shanghai Gardens and the Shear Magic Salon,
I found *Dave's Monuments* and imagined Dave like others
I'd met in the business, sharp-featured and bloodless.
I was wrong. He rounded the corner of the house, his shock
of blond hair, moustache to match, cheeks flushed. Carhartt
jacket and Timberland boots looked more Northwest Territories
than northeast funereal. Dave took off a work glove, held
out his hand, it was warm. I followed him through stacked
slabs of granite to a shed, where we sat on folding chairs
in front of an easel with newsprint tacked to a board. Both
quiet, not much to say. With a dark pencil he traced the sweep
of a curve, top of the headstone, its straight sides, then gave it
three dimensions. He scribbled grass around its base. I imagined
him an artist, a sculptor maybe, who needed a steady paycheck,
couldn't stomach working for someone else. I pictured us side
by side in a life drawing class, both lost in the curves of a body.
Dave offered me water, filled a glass from a pitcher. *What else
would you like?* He said, and for a moment, I wondered –
but he meant *on the stone*. In caps, he wrote my last name,
then below, my husband's first and middle, his dates of birth
and death. *What about him would you like to call out?* Maybe
his high-pitched laugh when he was surprised. Could you
capture that in stone? Or the energy he could contain until just
the right moment. How do you translate that to rock, my
monument maker? I leafed through his book of designs –
hearts, birds, a sailboat, masks of comedy and tragedy.
He was a publisher, I said, *how about a book and a pen?
And a fish? He loved the outdoors.* Dave hummed while
he sketched an open book, pen laying across the page.
Pine boughs at the corners. Artistic license. *He used to light*

the menorah with our son. Dave tucked a menorah into the boughs, added a Star of David. I wanted to rest my head on this man's shoulder. He reminded me of other places: the West, my younger self, my father at his easel. We did not finish, so I'd come back to see him again. Maybe it was the jacket, the boots, the stone, the cold.

Naming the Animals

Joan Mazza

for John L. Stanizzi

When in flight, geese are called a skein.
At rest, a gaggle. When they fly in a V,
they're a wedge. Not cheese, and not a flock.

A group of owls is a parliament, whose eyes
tell us this makes sense, unlike those crows perched
and cawing above the compost called a murder.

I hear *skein* and think of my mother asking me
to hold my hands up like the surgeon she wished
I'd grow up to become, not a wordsmith weaving

skeins of phrases. She wound wool into balls
to be knitted into sweaters with sturdy twisting cables.
The Brooklyn gangs were not elks, nor were

unemployed mobs filled with kangaroos.
Right here in Virginia, you'll see scurries
of squirrels more often than a skein of Canada geese.

Oh, but the frisson at their barking, as if
encouraging each other through winter skies,
wings rowing across the high deep blue,
shouting secrets both profound and true.

By the Numbers

Buffy Shutt

1 2 3 4 5 6 7 8 9 10
11 12 13 14 15 16 17 18 19 20
21 22 23 24 25 26 27 28 29 30
31 32 33 34 35 36 37 38 39 40
41 42 43 44 45 46 47 48 49 50
51 52 53 54 55 56 57 58 59 60
61 62 63 64 65 66 67 68 69 70
71 72 73 74 75 76 77 78 79 80
81 82 83 84 85 86 87 88 89 90
91 92 93 94 95 96 97 98 99 100
101 102 103 104 105 106 107 108 109 110
111 112 113 114 115 116 117 118 119 120
121 122 123 124 125 126 127 128 129 130
131 132 133 134 135 136 137 138 139 140
141 142 143 144 145 146 147 148 149 150
151 152 153 154 155 156 157 158 159 160
161 162 163 164 165 166 167 168 169 170
171 172 173 174 175 176 177 178 179 180
181 182 183 184 185 186 187 188 189 190
191 192 193 194 195 196 197 198 199 200
201 202 203 204 205 206 207 208 209 210
211 212 213 214 215 216 217 218 219 220
221 222 223 224 225 226 227 228 229 230
231 232 233 234 235 236 237 238 239 240
241 242 243 244 245 246 247 248 249 250
251 252 253 254 255 256 257 258 259 260
261 262 263 264 265 266 267 268 269 270
271 272 273 274 275 276 277 278 279 280
281 282 283 284 285 286 287 288 289 290
291 292 293 294 295 296 297 298 299 300

301 302 303 304 305 306 307 308 309 310
311 312 313 314 315 316 317 318 319 320
321 322 323 324 325 326 327 328 329 330
331 332 333 334 335 336 337 338 339 340
341 342 343 344 345 346 347 348 349 350
351 352 353 354 355 356 357 358 359 360
361 362 363 364 365 One year.

April 25, 2024 Day 793

Сімсот дев'яносто три (Ukrainian)
Семьсот Девяносто Три (Russian)

Ukrainian nonprofit Mizhvukhamy has archived 500 inscriptions left by Russian soldiers. 1

Sorry for the mess, but it's okay, Americans will help you clean up.

---

1   Hyperallergic.com

The Rabbit Dies

Sara Eddy

The vet tells me rabbits
are her worst patients, says
it's like they want to die.
That's so sad it's funny.
But later I think about
how loosely we hold on
to this fragile earth,
how easily our bodies
sigh and release us.
I had a cat that died
in my arms, once,
and I cried at how
gracefully she flew.
So when the dog
kills a rabbit in the yard
I try to think of it as a gift
that leaves blood
on his handsome fur
and lets the rabbit go.
It's not, of course,
but it lets me forgive him.

Afterlife

Ruth Smullin

Quotes from a NYT video published 2.12.24

I watch the video again and again, the girl's face
unsmiling as she speaks, eyes open wide, her lashes
exclamation points.

I heard my name. So I woke up.
And then I heard someone say
that her entire family was killed.
And I said "Me?"
Hands fly to her chest.

"Yes, that's you."
She shakes her head.
"No, my parents didn't die.
They're still here."

Her hands are quiet now.
Her voice trembles, pleading.
I said "You're liars. You're lying to me.
They weren't killed. They're alive."

The video cuts to mountains of rubble after a missile attack,
to a hospital where she lies in a coma, and back
to the living room where she sits in her wheelchair.

I was in a coma for fifteen days.
I couldn't remember anything that happened to me.
I couldn't remember my name or anything else.
I only remembered that maybe I saw my dad in front of me
before he was killed.

Everyone in the house was killed

**Eyes on her interviewer, she names the dead – her mother,
her father, her little brother,** all her grandparents, all her uncles
on her father's side and their wives and children, all her uncles
on her mother's side and their wives and children – as their smiling
photos fill my screen.

There were many children.
The house was full.
They were all killed.

She sighs deeply, looks down.

Hands in her lap, eyes red, she's crying
as she interrogates her interviewer.

She's interrogating me.

Why aren't we like the other children?
I would really like to understand.
I would really like to understand why they do this to us.
Because people can't live without their parents.

Effigy

Laurin Becker Macios

Night, cliffside knoll. I watch the tide controlled
by moon's invisible tether. Catch a wish I toss
on the tide's behalf, that it could move

of its own volition. How fucked. How dumb. What
desire am I projecting, the world unleashed? Gossamer
everything, decisions cut clean. I am opaque. I am

sad. I say so out loud, finger the tiny word, a sphere
I expect to snap in half. It dissolves like lavender
bath-bombed beneath a faucet. With two sharp stones

I make a blade, empty myself: funeral effigy carved
from a single piece of skin. I take care to paint myself lifelike:
crushed hydrangea, dried astilbe. Astilbe means

I'll wait for you. I fill my whittled body with it,
pestle apologies in the mortar of my skull.

A Gymnast Relives

Eric Braude

Wood rings dangle,
hand-chalk puffs in clouds.
I jump, catch, suspend,
my legs no longer logs. Wait

for wrist to marry ring.
Press to handstand, stare
at mat, rotate stick-straight torso,
point my toes. I'm in real tights,

not the floppy substitute
my family scrimped to buy. Raise
my shoulders, arms unbent,
become a cross, still.

Release. Fling everything
into one ascendant twisting flight.
My parents, freed from constant work,
attend this time, front row.

Gifts from My Father

Mark Walsh

An uncompromising need to walk among trees
        And live near the ocean;

Half a large array of his Craftsman tools;

Four neckties for all occasions;

One first edition of his anxiety;

One battered, incomplete birdwatcher's life list;

Five worn-out Louis Armstrong albums;

Uncountable hours in the family car
        Driving to Saturday errands;

The beneficiary yield
        On a five-year investment in psychotherapy;

One copy of the Collected Poems of Robert Service
        Wrapped in clear cellophane by my librarian mother;

A solid understanding that it's better to play sports than watch them
        Although watching sports can be fun, too;

Two sturdy, well-used chessboards
        The bigger board being the one
            He made with his large array of Craftsman tools;

One serviceable pair of binoculars
>   For watching undisturbed birds;

One innated sense of stability
>   With a life-time guarantee;

One tattered copy of his wit;

One reliable Pre-Kennedy Assassination Parker fountain pen
>   That creates my Post-Truth lines;

Three lucid hours of conversation
>   Before cancer ended his life;

An established method of wrapping your arms around your wife
>   While she cooks
>   Pressing your belly against her back
>   And smelling her hair;

An undying understanding that this life is worth your enthusiasm.

Why I Am Not Aging

Stephen Kampa

Either it's all the green tea
or it's the blood of the Nephilim
I keep in crystal bottles
tucked in the back of the closet.
I hardly bother reading
the glossy articles promising me
whiter teeth or rejuvenated
skin. Look at my neck: sagless,
unwattled. Look at my chin:
only the first few sparklets
of gray. Yes, I've heard the one
about the painting in my attic,
ditto the litany of bêtises
about backyard sacrifice –
honey, there aren't enough
chickens in the world
to keep a face looking like this!
Not that I wouldn't
sacrifice anything I had to.
You show me what I need
to destroy, and I'll show you
a man who'll live forever.

When my husband on our wedding anniversary

Laurel Benjamin

leans across the table at the hole-in-the-wall restaurant
and says *the tamale's all herbs* and puts his forks down,

I say *mine's plump*, legions of pork falling away
from crumbly masa. The owner approaches,

finger on lips, *beware of the chili*, like a prayer,
as if she could provide the marriage safe passage.

She sees beyond multi-color flags and laminated wood tables
to our kiss, tips of the lips. Walking home,

our steps, once an embrace, now a precipice.
I think of Romeo and Juliet, of Verona,

near the market, off a side street crammed with tourists,
where one-at-a-time, someone stands on the balcony

and yells down to a beloved or a friend pretending
to be a beloved. Because aren't we all Juliet?

Her story, seeking the friar, combining all the seasons
into her clouded heart. What tips would she dispense right now –

*go to the sea, check an easy-to-read inspiration pamphlet,
worship God not magic* – or are her secrets lost?

Now I dress for all eventualities, could survive in the woods,
choose berries for ink, because didn't my people

survive off manna in the desert forty years? The truth is
I haven't learned to harvest acorns, yet I climb the hills

where natives once lived, find a grinding stone to reveal
the seed inside the fruit, where flour leached in a stream

removes bitterness, where a sheltered camp means
the blue silk of an oak with long reaching branches.

Skinship

Tom Laughlin

for D

Beacon Street made way
for us walking this evening

to the bookstore. Inside we
take our seats in the crowd

spaced for social distance.
The venerable poet steps

to the podium. Her new poems
grab and weave through

Paris streets, into smoky
Beirut cafés of exiles

and refugees, past Shawarma,
Jambon-beurre, cups of Haleeb

Ma' Hal. But the afterwarmth
of you is fading. My hand

wants your fingers, the warmth
of your lower back curving,

curving against me.

Big Sur

Ed Gaudet

This poem has traveled
a long way to you:
Over mountains of ragged doubt,

through dense rose-blanketed briar, under fogged canopy of Life-Kings breathing out your name,

splashing
across the Agapao River.

Dark Forest, what is the meaning of love?

Look, the condor soars, stretches out love's size for you.

Dark Forest, how does love grow?

See, fiddleheads unfold love's beauty to you.

A coastal beauty, what is that?

A bridge
suspended in time
that connects love's span

over hairpin-carved creek
over sky-yellow sorrel, coltsfoot
over unseeable distance

and then climbing up the Earth's face
before dinner at the Post Ranch Inn.

So Much Depends

Brian Mosher

So much depends on where
you stand, which direction you face,
how strong the wind, how fair the skies.

So much is determined by timing,
by when you begin, and with whom,
the season, the phase of the moon.

So much rides on one roll of the dice,
a spin of the wheel, on who
marked the cards and who deals.

Your future can change in an instant,
redirected by something as small as
the scent of her hair, the color of her eyes.

The face you choose to hold in the
diamond of your mind is the fulcrum
upon which you balance yourself,

so, choose wisely, and never
underestimate the importance
of how well your hand fits inside another's.

Japanese Beetle

Claire McMillan

Bending to pluck a jewel of a beetle from the heart of a rose,
I spy a Scrabble tile in the grass.
The letter O, worth only one point.

Without O,
there is no joy,
but also no loss.
No atonement,
but no remorse.

Keep at it, beetle in that plush bed,
laying waste to love.

Cupid's spade

Ruchi Acharya

His arms, my deep chats
The cupid's spade is sharpened
to dig up my grave

Making Babies

Zvi A. Sesling

In Alytus, Lithuania a centuries old legend persisted that a woman who wanted to have a baby with the best traits of her mother or other ancestors needed to conceive in Alytus City Cemetery on the banks of the Nemunas River. Since it is too cold from October through April for this kind of activity, May to September is considered the optimum time, particularly July and August when the weather at night is warmest. The caveat to these months, however, is that the Alytus City Cemetery is on the banks of the Nemunas River which causes fog to engulf the cemetery on very warm evenings. This causes dew to form on the grass and the same legend holds that the dew is the sweat of the dead ones gone to the heat of the underworld. It is not recommended to attempt conception on such a night. On the night of August 9 Jakobas and Ugne Adomaitis enter the fog shrouded Ayltus City Cemetery, spread a blanket on the dew-covered grass above Ugne's mother's grave and remove their clothing in preparation for the conception of their first child. They are never seen again.

Night Swim

Karen Poppy

for Robert

Who could blame them?
Impregnated air – star jasmine,
Magnolia, summer rose bloom.
Swelter thick-tangled, boom
Of fireworks from nearby fair.

He, long in long board shorts,
More colt than stallion, alerts
Her that the coast is clear.
She, in bright bikini, a lanky mare.
Planets swirl, two jets pump light

On parallel course across sky
To twin destinations, while
Stars with locked divinations
Chart our course, determine
Our lives, our rise and fall.

To reach my pool, both kids jump
Over vined fence. Startle and jump
When they see me swimming within
This large, under-lit, undulating jewel.
Milky blue brine of it. My movement

Slow, purposeful, methodical.
Their laughs, nervous, wild –
Young and caught, nowhere
To go, so I invite them in.
Tell them I will leave soon.

She wastes no time, plunges
At deep end. He descends
Stairs at shallow, thinking
Of danger, what he calls sin,
Strike and burn within him.

"My mom told me to use protection.
'I don't want to raise more children!'
She said, he warns her once they meet
In exact middle, step-floating, embrace
Around waists, as if at a school dance.

I continue to swim, back and forth,
An interloping fish in my own pool.
Ears starting to waterlog, saturated birth
Of my own thoughts, drawn-out, gradual
And inevitable. Toward us – how we

Left it, how you will always be
Older, a logical and geographical
Impossibility. In backstroke to wall,
I scan sky for Venus, but only find Mars.
Fights and distance, emptied drawers.

Suddenly, both teens emerge.
She pushes him in at deep end,
But he swims over to shallow.
Contains his urge to invite her
Back in, hops out and towels off.

They leave. Still thinking, I continue my swim,
Intrepid mare like her, boy coward like him.
A drowned bee hits my hand, floats away
Like any possibility of us, days of pollen
To flower, nectar to honey – dead and over.

For trying to love each other,
Who could blame us? Nights
Like tonight were ours too.
Impregnated air – star jasmine,
Magnolia, summer rose bloom.

At the Lake

Beth Boylan

that final Sunday of summer, you snuck us past the *Members Only* sign
to the line of canoes tied up & bobbing against the dock. We exhaled

& kissed with the arrogance of thieves, dipped our feet in the circling
minnows. We dove off the edge to the rocky bottom, dove into each
other

as the last carload left the parking lot; your skin tasted like melon
& the air after rain. You sucked the knob of my shoulder

& the breath from my lungs – when your hands touched my thighs,
I could have walked on water. As the sun slid behind the houses

on the opposite shore, we watched the sky turn the shade
of blackberries & the blue smoke of barbecues.

We laughed & swore to love, to forever,
swore to keep swimming straight into fall,

right through the deep end – choosing to ignore
any dangers ahead and the cold ache of dusk.

Ode to Frank O'Hara's Hands

Beth Boylan

Mine grasp a Diet Coke and show their age tonight,
chapped from a long winter, hangnails chewed to the quick.
My father once said I have the hands of a pianist,
but any elegance is long gone. O, Frank,
how my hands have fumbled –
on the page, for a lover's breasts, in desperate prayer –
I think of yours so often:
scribbling on the 4:19 to East Hampton
or trimming wisteria from a ladder,
cigarette in one, half-filled glass in the other –
paintbrush, pen, or penis, O! –
splattering paint on the rubber tips of your sneakers
or tossing back a string of cognacs
when your sculptor friend died; even then,
gorgeous in their trembling.
Even on that late July evening, when you lay broken
in the Fire Island sand, and they purpled in the glow of headlights,
O, how they must have unfurled and fought for more –
all the words left to scrawl,
just one more shot of gin and tangerine to peel,
just one more chance to burst out and punch the greenish light of day.
.

list poem

Jack Giaour

    fag
    /fag/ *noun*

    ancient fires fueled by heretical bodies
    his half-smoked pack of american spirit on the nightstand
    public obscenity trials
    moment to moment trending on snapchat
    he was a professional cremator before stonewall
    come away from the window   can we talk   ?
    he had the shakes he just needed a smoke
    old circus mentality
    minds and bodies at the witches' feet
    it's been an unseasonably warm summer for this part of the state
    would you mind ?   i ask for a lighter   *my head is pounding*
    who started the fires in the rainforest   ?
    his fierce voice
    who detonated the bombs over palestine   ?
    from the old english   meaning "a man on fire"

Hookus

Robert Carr

Not a dictionary word. I searched.
Family slang for boy parts,

something like a shame flushed cheek,
an exclamation, dirty to be

cleaned, *Wash your hookus!*
Put away your hookus! (Her voice

is diamond through an earlobe.)
Jiggly, blood-stained tighty-whities,

thumb pressed to the roof
of Bea's house. I'm guessing twisted

Yiddish, *tuchus*, ass, picked up
on Annapolis streets.

Upward pointing flesh, Baryshnikov's
pale tights, ovaries on the outside.

Mr. Bubble, gum scented;
Bubbles kids clean...

softens skin. Imperfection to be cut,
divining rod in whirlpools,

dreamscape in rooms on Duke
of Gloucester, boy without a root.

It's a Risk to Write About Sex

Robin Dellabough

In a naked yoga class, I try not to look
at men's dangles as they dance into positions.
I remember walking east on a sliver of sand, suddenly
naked men were walking west. I looked straight at them
but that wasn't anything like sex. These days, the men wear
penis cozies, against sunburn I suppose. Women
don't worry about their tender insides being exposed.
I've had two abortions. Didn't stop me. I've had sex
in phone booths, on boulders, sailboats, soccer fields,
golf courses, kitchen counters, in tents, airplanes,
basements, bathrooms, backseats. Beaches
seemed romantic with the high school boy I loved
but sand and sand flies left skin raw, itchy. We were reckless
about where our young limbs landed. My sister says
I taught her about "healthy" sex. She was confused
by our father's *Playboys,* as if those overblown women
were sexy. I can't name the best sex but I know
when it turned out to be the last. Years ago. Now I read romance
novels. Still dream of naked men. Kissing one man: pure sex.

Nightstand

Adam Grabowski

If one plays their grace where it finds them then even the heartfelt
hairy torso of a half-stranger can feel like home. If only for a second
could we tell each other *yes* & still each pull, each push forward

yields a second more. Yes, there's no found calm in this permission
though here I am unfolding myself being unfolded garment-by-garment;
there you are turning onto your stomach *here, this way*. Your child surrendered,

your marriage opened, for a time your quiet, wild mouth, your natural grief,
  finds a home here.

a/sunder

Sandra Fees

       isn't divorce / a tincture for the scald
       of blame / and rebuff?

       isn't detachment / an unruly couplet / scythed?

       after sorrow slackens / shred the brackish
       covenant / compose a solitary line –

                            a lone sparrow.........

Where do I go from here?

Elly Guzikowski

Damp mountain air,
quiet of a home untouched
by other peoples homes.
Each morning I stand
outside for 3 minutes,
just breathing.
One hand in my pocket,
the other spinning
the hair at the base
of my neck.
I wait for today to touch me.
The dawn is warm
like pulling yourself from
sleep, sweaty and slack jawed
in rosette underwear
a ripped t-shirt.
Days are flying past me
each wide open,
aching sunrise
swallowing this summer.
Hailing my return to city smog,
young filth with distracted hands,
boys that don't seem to notice
the rotting smell of my body
falling to pieces.

Improv Student Showcase

Jon Wesick

The green room roars.
"Seven things! Seven things! Seven things!"
Improv students clap to the rhythm.
Stan leads us in a warrior chant.
"We will crush their bones with humor!
Drink applause from their skulls!"

Past inspirations decorate wooden beams
in black magic marker. "Stay golden, Ponyboy."
"Fail! Fail better!"

Bodies bump backstage.
Then fists pumping to some disco tune,
we dance onto the stage. Like an interrogation
from a film noir, bright lights hide
the audience in darkness. A Zen master
would face this with mind a dustless mirror,
but the Kentuckian samurai I imagine obsesses me.

Fear is in the waiting, not the doing.
"They laughed at me at the university
but from this lump of inanimate flesh
I have created   Martha Stewart!"
We play with living scenery, sweep edits,
scene crashes, and call backs; get a few laughs.
"Look, I taught this squid to read braille!"

At the after party, Marco's laughter echoes
from courtyard walls while Rachel strikes poses
in a pantsuit with shoulder pads. For me
only the bones of reality –
lonely subway ride, parking garage,
gray cement under artificial lights.

Out of nowhere, love
swells in my chest, love
for the lawyers returning from a banquet, love
for the woman arguing about Gouda over a cell phone, love
for the janitor sweeping a deserted platform

Explaining "the patron saint of suicide"[1]

Matthew E. Henry

I generally dissociate during poetry readings. Tonight is no different. I explain this to the audience after the event's organizer reads a kind, but way too long introduction full of embarrassing accolades. I slink up to the mic behind the bookstore's branded lectern, thank her, and avoid eye contact while telling them I won't really be present, won't have any idea what I've said or done when they ask me specific questions while I'm signing books, while making small talk over precariously balanced cups of wine and plates of cheese and crackers. As long as no one farts loudly during a quiet moment,
I'll be in my own world on stage. It usually gets a
laugh. Of course I'm 95% serious.

* * * * *

Clinically, dissociation is described as having an out-of-body experience or feeling like a different person. You have gaps in your memory. You're emotionally numb, detached. You don't notice pain. The physical world flits away – is not as real, as present, as it previously was, as real as they tell you it *should* be. All this tracks. A therapist once told me I'm not really disassociating. She might have been right. But when friends ask me how a reading went, it's a legitimate struggle to cobble together memories of anything coherent to share. Unless something noteworthy happened: the college girls who stomped out in a huff; the old white guy who wrapped a wrinkled arm, and his thoughts on how I could be a better Black man, around my shoulders; the karen who wanted to know what right I had sharing my own painful experiences to a roomful of strangers; my very religious parents walking in while I read a poem about faith and bad sex. Every reading I guard against being overwhelmed. I retreat into the story, crouch behind the speaker of the poem, even if that speaker is only a slightly-fictionalized version of myself. The audience isn't seeing, hearing, me. They get "MEH": the stage version of me. The *staged* version of me. And for good reason – shit can get real otherwise and no one has time for that.

*****

During the pandemic, through email, social media, and poetry readings on Zoom, I became friends with Joan Kwon Glass. She was easily one of the most talented poets I met during that time, so I didn't hesitate to buy her book, How to Make Pancakes for a Dead Boy. Her words are always profound and moving, but I wasn't fully prepared for this collection. Each poem struck a chord in my heart – some ringing too familiar – before tearing out the strings and smashing the instrument on the concrete. Midway through the book I read "Googling the Patron Saint of Suicides" – Joan's record of the horrors faced by the martyrs Saint Rita of Casia and Saint Dymphna, as well as three girls from her childhood church who were raped by their father, the respected choir director. Her poem asks many perennial questions – "*Why do horrible things happen?*," "*How do people survive here?*" –, but ends with one my grad school training in theology made me think I could answer: "*Where is the saint who refuses forgiveness?*" Through tears, I penciled into the margin, "technically, Jonah." I placed her book atop the pile beside my bed, lifted a disused notebook and pen from the nightstand, and began drafting a response.

41

My intent was never to do a deep dive into the enslavement, torture, and murder of eighth century Jews, but that all became important context to cover. It's the reason the prophet Jonah's story begins with a silent "fuck off" in response to YHWH's call to deliver a message to his ethnic enemies, his people's oppressors. It's why he hops on a ship heading toward Spain, as if YHWH can't *hables español*. My first year teaching, my freshmen read Jonah's story as a companion piece to *The Odyssey*. After we went into detail about the racism and racial conflicts at its heart, a lightbulb went off in Christina's blue-eyed head. She told the class that

> ...Jonah's mission
> was equivalent to God sending my Black ass to hand out
> Gospel tracts at a cross burning.

She wasn't wrong. This is Jonah's mindset – the reason he had the sailors toss him overboard, spent three days in the belly of a big fish, delivered a false message to his oppressor's capital city, defied YHWH in the first place and repeatedly thereafter. He wasn't damning the consequences, he was welcoming them, daring his God to act. Jonah wanted to die. He said so in chapter 4, verse 3. So there's Jonah, the suicidal prophet, refusing to offer forgiveness.

"the patron saint of suicide" is ekphrastic. As such, I borrowed from Joan's poem – the "impossible," "a difficult marriage," swarming "white bees," but placed her questions about surviving the horrific into the mouths of my students. They are the things they ask me as their process their own lives, their own dark thoughts. Hurts born of their families, friends, their own minds and bodies. I did not intend for to bring myself into view – possibly another form of disassociating –, but I looked down to find I had compared myself to Jonah, admitting

> ... of the many times I contemplated
> seeing my reflection from the other side of a frozen lake,
> or the Basquiat beauty of speed and an apt guardrail
> hovering over a sleeping bridge, none of my reasons
> have ever been as noble, as honorable as his. or

      as utilitarian. the greatest good for the greatest number
      of his people.

One could pretend this is about the veneration of racial martyrdom discussed later in the poem – a holy laying down of one's life for a greater cause – but we know better.

I also know how publishing works – the odds were good that no one would ever read these words, no magazine would ever accept them – so what was the harm in writing the truth? But just in case I sent a draft to Joan for thoughts, critique, or shutting the whole endeavor down. No editor would read a line without the blessing she graciously gave. After it was published, and I began to read it publicly, kind-eyed women began expressing concern for my kids – my students – while my own confessions were often too steep to raise their eyes or voices. Not that it matters: I barely noticed their praise or discomfort when blissfully below the waves with Jonah.

* * * * *

The reading is going as well as expected. It's graciously attended by friends, both personal and of poetry. The poets who read earlier in the night had kept the audience captivated with jealous-making selections. I'm last up for the night and reading from my newest collection, *said the Frog to the scorpion*, which includes "the patron saint…" in its final form. I generally read it nearing the end of my set.

43

It's longer than most of my poems, and its content departs from the game the audience is asked to play hearing each poem: "Step right up and divine if this poem is about working in a predominantly white (and racist) public school system, or a romantic relationship with an equally toxic and unstable white woman? Door #1 or Door #2?!" I give a brief explanation of the poem's inspiration, encourage the audience to buy Joan's work, then read.

* * * * *

As the poem begins, I mime how

> ...the assyrians wedged unsanded wood under ribs
> and full body weight, sliced thin strips from thighs,
> cheeks...,

my fist leaning into an impaled chest, hand taunt into a sharp, blood slick blade. It's all pre-planned, practiced, so thinking is only required in the emergency of responding to the people in front of me. Dialing up or down some element to better pierce a heart with my words. But even then, all the possible permutations of the audience have been accounted for. At least in theory.

I've learned a lot on the stages I've crossed in my life as part of dramatic performances, in bands, at conferences and churches. Being a high school and college educator has helped as well. There are ways to deliver words. A craft beyond merely speaking, reciting, or reading. Moving past the strained "poet's voice" mocked in most movies – the hackneyed image of a poorly shaven white dude in a black turtleneck with a beret atop his unkempt, greasy hair, accompanied by bongo drums and snapping fingers from under a haze of hookah smoke and patchouli oil. It's about knowing when to raise your voice and lower it. When to pause for laughter or a proffered gasp. The slowing and speeding of pace. Slurring or over-enunciating as appropriate. Being comfortable with the physical embellishments that must punctuate an image, an element of the narrative, or the actions of a character.

But sometimes that's not enough distance from some audiences. I uncharacteristically pause at the end of the stanza explaining how

> antebellum plantation owners of the American South

practiced on their slaves what the Assyrians preached centuries before, and glance up. I see the faces before me and suddenly remember who is in the room. Damn it.

This is my first mistake.

According to some coworkers and other naysayers, students should know nothing of my struggles with depression and suicidal ideation. I generally tell them how and where to most painfully shove their opinions. Honesty with my kids is paramount, especially about this.

How is stigma addressed if everyone is too terrified to talk about it? There's enough silent suffering. I've seen the impact on those unwilling to do so. I want them to know they're not alone, to get the help they need, to see a future with them in it is possible. To hope. I often present the question in class: what's the worst that could happen being honest with a trusted adult or friend? Ask them to consider how outrageously pitiful a person would have to be to come at them with negativity because they have admitted to working on their mental health. I usually remember that I'm not legally allowed to use certain words to describe such a villain in a public school setting. However, questioning whether there is a broad history of matrilineal incest, or a family's propensity to fornicate with the myriad livestock of the American Midwest readily comes to mind.

* * * * *

My gaze drops back to the book in my hands. It's not like I can stop reading so close to the end, but it's tempting. What I can do is sink back below the surface. It's peaceful there. Less complicated. I take a breath and begin to mentally chat a new mantra: *Don't look up. Don't look up. Don't look up. Don't look up. Don't look... Fuck.*

My second mistake.

It's hard to disassociate after meeting multiple sets of eyes. The eyes of kids I had in heart while writing this poem. Seeing, feeling, the moments held in those eyes. When I held her crying outside my classroom door. When he casually told me one morning before school that I'm the reason he's still alive. When I used a pair of safety scissors to cut the ID bracelet from her wrist after she was released from the psych ward. When I questioned their long sleeves and cargo pants in 80° weather. When she asked after class one day, *"not everyone feels like this* all *the time?"* When I had to call their home after receiving their "goodbye" letter via email. When I was forced to send the police to their door. It's hard to dissociate when the scale for how bad are you doing? isn't 1 to 10, but sarcasm to silence. When I can still hear all the dark jokes we've shared, along with the meaning of when the laughter stopped. When I remember their worries that the ceiling would collapse if anyone knew the truth. Worries about being seen walking into the adjustment counselor's office. Worries about what their friends would think, what their families would think. Stupid worries about being a burden, taking up too much space, too much of my time, being dramatic, or making a big deal out of nothing. It's hard to disassociate when eyes all around the room – front row right to back center left – are filling or spilling with tears. Tears for themselves, for me. Including those with the knowledge that I am, right now, grieving a recent loss to suicide. It's hard to disassociate when my own eyes seem to be leaking, are screeching across the room, the faces, the page, the lines. And, somehow, I still have to finish this Goddamn last stanza and the rest of the reading.

It's been half a breath. Far too long a pause. A fraction of a fraction of a second, but still, I take another breath and finish reading the poem. I will my mind elsewhere. It lands a week ago when he pulled me into a side room and asked me how I've stayed alive so long? And why I bother? And what's the point? Before the bookstore's crowd my mouth is full of the truth I told him – what I've told them all, what I tell myself:

> *we hold onto whatever keeps us going until*
> *something better comes along, and then*
> *we hold on to that.* but sometimes, like them,
> I would rather not.

---

1 "the patron saint of suicide" was originally published in *Cola Literary Review Vol 2.*
Quotes from the poem are indented in the text of this narrative.
Images are details from a 16th Century woodcut, artist unknown.

the patron saint of suicide

Matthew E. Henry

"...it is better for me to die than to live!"
~ *The Book of Jonah 4:3b*

question:
where is the saint who refuses forgiveness?

answer:
in the Book of Jonah a man ran away from a God
who, when asked, *why do horrible things happen?*
answered, *they are Mine. I can do what I want
with them — even save them.* a prophet who knew God
could forgive everything. a victim who thought
such grace, such mercy, to be utter bullshit.
the assyrians wedged unsanded wood under ribs
and full body weight, sliced thin strips from thighs,
cheeks, and so amused themselves with amputations,
antebellum plantation owners studied their zeal
centuries later. he'd rather die than see them saved.
and I get it.

stalked by a difficult marriage, caring for impossible
cases, afflictions swarming like white bees in
and out of my mouth... of the many times I contemplated
seeing my reflection from the other side of a frozen lake,
or the Basquiat beauty of speed and an apt guardrail
hovering over a sleeping bridge, none of my reasons
have ever been as noble, as honorable as his. or
as utilitarian. the greatest good for the greatest number
of his people. a Christ-figure frustrated by a big fish
and promises to pay what he had vowed. I get that too.

my first year teaching, a student said Jonah's mission
was equivalent to God sending my Black ass to hand out
Gospel tracts at a cross burning. I nodded at her profundity.
said something along the lines of *fuck that noise*
in my heart. given the choice, I too would choose the sea
for the sake of my skin – my people. I would choose –
like him – to be buried beside the ancestors who jumped
from the Master's ship. but nothing is certain. survival happens
despite our best efforts. in the end, Jonah remained
angry enough to die. but he remained.

while suffering their own afflictions – often
familial, always familiar – my students ask,
how do people survive here? when "forgive"
and "forget" are two sides of the unflipped coin
clenched in their fist. my most honest answer –
I have no idea – floods my dammed mouth
as I search their faces for something
that might be useful. instead I say – I believe –
*we hold onto whatever keep us going until
something better comes along, and then
we hold on to that.* but sometimes, like him,
I would rather not.

after "Googling the Patron Saint of Suicides" by Joan Kwon Glass

In Summer

Jacqueline Coleman-Fried

If I want to drive to the beach, as I always do,
   you don't want to go.

If I need to drive to the mountains to escape
   a heat wave, you don't want to.

If I yearn to fly some place we've never seen
   to enlarge our view of the world,
   you say, Go by yourself.

I wake each day in the same
   drape-darkened room, door closed
   to hold the cooled air.

Walk the same paths and streets,
   walk the same streets and paths.

Shop, as always, at Trader Joe's.
   Broil salmon, as per usual.

Only seasonal fruit – brief
   cherries and peaches –
   perk me up.

Fun, too, when I think about it –
   my legs in Bermudas. Swimming
   in the backyard pool.

Drinking an Arnold Palmer
    under a sun umbrella,
    the smell of SPF 70,

the hat that makes me look
    like Lawrence of Arabia.
    Giddy pink lipstick.

And our garden, darling,
    blooming like cancer
    in the longest light.

Cantata for Chemo Infusion Pack
Neal Silberblatt

This device to which I am tethered –
its umbilical cord anchored to a port
below my right clavicle –
hums
wordlessly.

Like Gould humming along
to Bach's Partita No. 1 in B-flat major
as though he had forgotten
the words.

The slow pernicious humming
as the pump
slowly drips
drips
its toxins into my bloodstream.

This relentless sostenuto mimics the notes
played by Uchida's left hand
in the first movement of Schubert's Piano Sonata No. 21 –
also in B-flat major –
the one he never got to hear
before he died at 31.

Yet, even now, I wait for the
moment that my device –
or Gould or Uchida –
will burst into song,
perhaps a few bars of *Wachet Auf* or *Ave Maria*.
It would make the poison
so much more palatable
and might alleviate the dread
of what may follow.

This Is Not a Ghazal

Rusty Barnes

Given a tooth to pull, I have a mouthful
of old ghazals to chew. They wrap tightly

my fey tongue, burnishing my teeth,
awaiting the dentist's next move,

preparation for the incursion, sharps
proffered, tiny knifepricks, painful

even through the numbing agents
swabbed between my cheek and gum.

My wife holds my ankle to calm me,
the only part of my body she can reach

while staying out of the surgeon's way.
Right now it's aces for the tongue –

lashing the bored attendant is taking
from a strange-named woman ahead

of me all silken-voiced and righteous.
Poems reveal themselves in due time.

Here I am, freshly numbed and cracked,
tooth pulled, waiting for my bank

to approve my purchase of healthy
mouth and, for the first ghazal to come.

Near Edmond, Oklahoma: August

Dale Cottingham

Halted, where she looks at the prairie grass,
long dry, fallow dry. One way, as I see it,
a self makes an allegory of the land: isn't
she like that, only a husk, having before
poured herself out,

fully, to-the-last measure, that kind of pouring.

Above her, the sun blares unprophetically, making
this one more day to get through, she thinks. There's
pain that's imposed

upon us. There's pain
that comes from inside, from what we did,
what we failed to do. She stands at roadside
for what seems like forever, lost in a name
she can't forget, that winnows its way
to the core, as if the memory of it was all it took
to further hollow her out, it's that kind of name.

The Year I Went Without Being Discovered

Mark DeCarteret

It was a retraction. An activity I now took to be uncalled for. Yet another fact, not anywhere near as much fun, as we had once thought. Then they went and scratched me off the cast listing. To make room for a limousine ad. And the souls of the actors who'd left us far too early. So now, in the first act, I'm only an apostle. This near-stop in play. And the last follower of Christ to wear head gear fashioned out of wool. Taste His blood in my soft drink. The tide so low, I could still see where the sandpipers had slowed down. Only to be gowned in the sun's light. Won over by giddiness. Where the shipwreck had repositioned itself. Long enough to be pecked at by the wind. And where I'd try to rinse that crosshair out of my eye. Though this still isn't a retraction. A square vacated by the piece of fluff that had come to rest there. Or another request, lacking the completed form, laughed off uncontrollably. While now, in the second act, I'm an understudy for Christ. The secret word the tech world lowered its character minimum. The next-in-line to bottom out. Be so outmoded I'm doomed. To tap into this tomb-like application again. The tide so high I can no longer see where the sandpiper passed his wand over the sand. And made several stripes. Followed by lots of dots. That would fail us as verse. Serving only to inspire us. To dig deeper with our shovels. Targeting the chill and the absence of life. With a love that is greater than all the hearts. Given a start by this performance. God knows, I need to do something different with my wardrobe.

Little Madam,

Susanna Rich

Mother calls me as I rattle through her
Avon sample lipstick box – ranks of reds,
pinks, purples in gold bullet tubes.
My mission – match her tight purple dress.

She parts her pale lips for the mirror,
strokes them with what she reads
for me – *Plum Delicious*.
I rub my lips with my dry finger,
blot with tissue, to be like her.

Farewell cheek to cheek,
not to smear her lips
glossed to a puckered heart.

I ask each time where she's going.
My business, she says,
doing what a mother must.
Really, it's all for you.

When I've watched her disappear
at the end of the block,
I pull off her lipstick caps,
stand them up, like red fingers reaching,

draw a face onto my belly –
Siren Song lips in an O around my navel,
Burnt Orange eyes around
my nipples, her colors
I cover with my blouse
when I dress myself in the morning.

The Oil Man Tells Me All About the Bobcat in His Yard

Rachel Becker

and pulls up a video of her bottom-heavy body,
sweeping haunches, nudging her litter
back into the reedy woods. A pounce of them
live there, on the land behind his house in Methuen.

The oil man – his name is Carl! Says he bleeds oil
and also? He's just being honest:
our tank's rusting out. It's not leaking. Yet.

Only the bobcat is news.

He shows me his wife in the video,
standing even closer to the bobcat!

He's filmed them both from behind,
their backs to the camera.

What does he want me to see? Is he flirting?
Or do my eye bags and tired hair just cry out,
please fix my furnace, and also, tell me a story?

Carl gathers his bucket and sack cloth
but lingers in the doorway. Were I a six foot four,
tattoo-sleeved man, he'd have left an hour ago.

But no. It's as if the soft-compact of me needs
his looking after. He doesn't know
I'm also a mother, a feral energy.

Sad Maryanne

Brad Rose

I'm a secret message to myself. According to the rules, the brain is made up of 86 billion cells. It doesn't matter if you're below sea level or above sea level; you can still have lots of ghost fun. Like a jelly fish or a glass of water, it's nearly see-through. Maryanne says that considering my modus operandi, I'm lucky as an uninhabited planet. She's an excellent mind reader. Yesterday, we were exchanging chemicals and talking about dinosaur angels. Sure, they existed, but now they're extinct. Maryanne says that's why they're not in the Bible anymore. Of course, you've got to make up your own mind about things, so I'm doing what I can to improve the neighborhood, like locking myself out of my house until I capture all my own emissions. I told Maryanne about the way things used to be around here – you know, peaceful, calm, and normal, like in the old days. And for no reason, just like that, she wept.

Silk

Grace Massey

– inspired by *The Book of Questions* by Pablo Neruda

Do you not know that the sea
is a silken scarf
that we walk this desert
on blooms of ancient coral
bleached fingers
beneath our feet?

Lover, do you know
the spider's silk will stop
a bullet, heal a wound? In Madagascar
seventy people toiled years
collecting spiders
from telephone poles, golden
filament to wrap the apples
of your breasts.

Yes, the female
wasp dies within
the fig, the blossom
dies within
the apple, you eat
their souls, spit the seeds
into your cupped hands.

Curb Appeal But Don't Open the Front Door

Jeffry Bernstein

My mother loved roast chestnuts,
preached their virtues. I first caught
their seductive aroma one smoky
second summer afternoon near
Central Park. I've tried to
understand their shiny appeal
but once autumn fades and
they've cooled enough to pop
one in my mouth, I just can't
keep it down, spit out masticated
mush into a napkin. Still, when
those glossy orbs emerge again
on the co-op shelves, I hear her
dinner bell ringing, summoning us home.

Horseshoes & Red Wine

John Dorsey

for mike james

every time we got together
we argued about ezra pound
& if you were here now
i would still tell you
he was as boring as a dense fog
but contrary to popular belief
it's the dead
who have the last word

i can still see you
sitting there at the local fair
laughing as they announced the winner
of the greased pig race
drinking cheap red wine
your heart as big as a hay bale
& that's what matters
not words flung like horseshoes
that never seem to reach
their intended targets
just you sitting there patiently
with dan up 3 days
off his meds
talking about how he was
never going to write poems again
while you squeezed his hand.

On the Tenth Anniversary of Our Ghosting,

Jennifer Martelli

I'm thinking of our very last conversation about those men who always come back.

They always come back, Jenn, you said. I'd watched a French film about the dead

who returned, came back, hungry, not for flesh: they just wanted to be home.

Nobody in the little Alpine town was happy about this.

The undead were dumb, became nuisances, roamed the cold mountain roads

      trying to remember what they did in life that made money or brought joy.

Rester mort! an old widower yelled to his wife who was trying to mend his shirt.

Even the butterflies pinned to a mat in his dusty study began to flutter, to twitch.

Sometimes, a relationship means more to one person than to the other.

Someone makes another person wait at the café or the bookstore.

Someone will wait.

This precarious balance is silent, necessary. No need to heal, to make up.

But if we do, I still have that old sweater I gave you and you left at my home.

Remember it? The forest green knit, the hole you burnt in the wool, the faux

fur collar? Which of us lost the yarn belt to hold it closed across the belly?

A Poem With Spoilers

Jennifer Martelli

Mia, forgive me, the rooms in my dream last night were yours –

I needed a toothbrush and rushed down your long hall, banging on cheap wood doors,

intruded on your Park Slope life, invented roommates and baggies full of pills I pray you don't have.

Perhaps I dreamt this because I'd read the story about a mother who slowly poisons her three

    girls with pills in their milk:

laxatives and tranquilizers ground fine as arsenic with a pestle.

The author describes the pills so beautifully: an unreal blue, like cleanser, like cotton candy on the tongue.

One daughter carves words into her body – she is the narrator – one daughter dies, one daughter

    kills other girls and takes their teeth.

Mia, I didn't read this story – it was read to me over the course of a day into my ears while I

    walked and washed and swept.

And then I dreamt myself into your life the other night: it was warm and there was no moon.

To Lunge a Horse

Cal Freeman

make a V of your right and left hand,
left hand gripping the lunge line
and right hand dangling the whip.
Give the horse enough rope to circle
around you in a 15-yard circumference.
Begin counterclockwise with the trot.
Begin counterclockwise as all cyclonic
storms north of the equator must begin.
If the horse tries to turn, reinvent
the circle's center while pointing the whip
at its flank; if the horse attempts
to kick you, lightly touch the whip
to its left hindquarter. When cuing it to canter,
raise the whip's tail and let it fall
softly near the rear fetlock gripping
the lunge line tight in case the animal flees;
brace yourself to be dragged if the knotted
end slips down to your left hand
lest the animal get in the habit
of galloping away and become
a barnstormer. Each hemisphere
of the equine brain learns separately.
If your horse has mastered
the counterclockwise trot and canter,
those skills will not translate
to the clockwise orientation. By "learn"
we might not mean learn exactly
but thoughtless acquiescence
to a thoughtless task; don't confuse
these inane details for wisdom.

This is all to say that one must repeat
the process in both directions and shouldn't
be alarmed when the animal spooks
at a benign object that has been added
to the scene. For to trot while eyeing
a rail of white out of the left eye
and processing it in the right brain hemisphere
is not the same as to trot while eyeing
a rail of white punctuated by a black
riding helmet a child has left behind.
We've seen several lose themselves to panic
when just the smallest detail's out of place.
Even when terrified of its untrammeled
beauty, do not let on. If the horse believes
in your performance, there will come a point
you're no longer worth the fight. Don't mistake
this companionship for friendship. What you've forged
through habit can only feel like love.

Landscapes of Silence

Sara Letourneau

The car is too quiet as the two of you drive along
Iceland's coast, thousands of miles from home.
He's at the wheel, and you're in the passenger seat,
wishing there was music, or wind from an open window,
something to distract you from the swelling urge of your tears.
There was no argument this morning,
but he has barely spoken since you left the hotel room,
where he snapped at you after you asked
whether to bring granola bars for the day trip.

Yes, he snapped at you – or so you believe.
He has never done this before, nor has he ever yelled
or sworn at anyone in the three years you've known him.
But as he drives, the absence of voices crackles
around you, and you're certain he hears it, too.
So certain that you don't ask for confirmation.
So certain that you wonder what you've done wrong,
and if he's pretending you're not there,
and why you keep stumbling over rocks
as you try to navigate this mapless land of love.

It reminds you of the times when your mother,
in a fit of wounded rage, would deem you responsible
for her feelings, and then ignore you.
For days, sometimes weeks, her energy would burn you
and the whole house, hot and wordless and unbearable,
even when you would beg for forgiveness,
even when you would tell her, *Good morning*.
And so you were trained
to wait for the other mouth to open first

and bide your time while blaming yourself.
Do you feel it, the same poisonous enmity, from him?
You want to say no. You want to believe
he's empty of words because he's as tired
from your eight days of travels as his face suggests.
But he says nothing
about the lava fields and rock formations,
nothing about the gray, softly raining day,
not even an *I love you*.
And so you say nothing, too.

Botany

Hannah Larrabee

for Joey Santore of *Crime Pays But Botany Doesn't*

The Latin isn't everything but it is precise,
and precision must be part of it, why else
would you tattoo a ruler on your finger?
You want to get it right, you speak to plants
in places rarely visited, and even if it's some
silphium prairie leaves or a little plump cactus
with spiny batteries sitting on a bed
of Cretaceous limestone, you see it for
what it is, I mean – how it got there, only
a thick Chicago accent tying you to one place;
motherfucker of a cactus that one right there
you say, and we try to look for what you see.
Echinocactus horizontilonius like a green apple,
quartered. Don't ask me, this isn't my world
though I love it. And how many desert sunsets
have you barely beat, or maybe you like to walk
the night amongst friends. The stars wait for you
to name them, too, but your head is turned down
to where there's no escaping the encroachment
we, as human beings, push and shove onto every
landscape. In this video, you spend some time
wondering about the iron-oxidized, sandblasted
stone seemingly out of place in this part of Texas.
Ventifact, you say, which is the word for something
as beautiful as a wind-faceted stone.

There Were so Many Fucking Whales

Karina Jutzi

We started to get suspicious.

We pictured a factory farm of krill underneath the hull.
Desperate sonic whistles calling them from across the sea.

Impossible to believe
in all the vastness of the ocean,
they would choose us.

They were the most beautiful things I'd ever seen &
yet I longed to be drunk.

Cynthia is dying.
Jonathan is getting married for the second time.
Heather has put the black dress back on
after all these years.

Whales breathe in a foreign language.
Spouts lifting out of the water in a sonic boom.

How can I tell them we were put on this Earth to destroy it?

That urge to put the antlers over the fireplace,
to rub a lightning bug's skin against your own,

so that for one second
you can glow.

Imagine what tree tells owl

Miriam O'Neal

Imagine what tree tells owl
early in the morning
as light opens its mouth
and begins its meal of night.

How to Leave

Michael Quattrone

Where would you go, except outside
yourself, that old agreement
of misremembered hurts.

After miles on a salted road,
anyone's boots will bring their sting
and stain into the house.

Step to a lit door.
Stomp off the accumulated grit.
Pretend the new place is home.

Nothing to blame but the wind
at your neck, the choice you made
to live on arrival.

Stay. Even the bluest snow
melts on your breath.

Reviews

A Review of Marble Dust by Gary Metras (Červená Barva Press)

Miriam O'Neal

Marble Dust is Gary Metras's twenty-third book. As Harris Gardner explains, "it is a travelogue in four parts. [ ] a paean to geography, actual, spiritual, historical, mythological as well as a special place in our collective hearts."

Metras leads the reader along streets in Milan, Florence, and Assisi as well as other cities in other countries, sometimes leaning too completely on the history of places. Several of the longer poems get swamped with facts and a prosiness that washes out the potential for music and/or the image under observation. However, that changes as we move further east through Vienna and on, to Sarajevo and later, back to the English Channel and deep into the 19th Century.

The magic begins with "Swimming With The Swans." What might have been a standard swans- on-pond scene is upended by the appearance of a swimmer who has slipped into the water and joined the great white birds in their paddling. The image is wonderfully unexpected and the shape of the poem on the page matches its subject. In the first part of the poem, the coupled lines pivot quickly, steering much as the indifferent swans in their approach and rejection of fans along the shore. The shift to more even lines in the second part evokes the swimmer as he strokes evenly and quietly among the birds

Reviews

before 'He paddles back/to shore, stands in dry air.../. The poems that follow from this point are more deftly crafted than the earlier travelogue poems. Here we ride a cable car up a mountain only to catch sight of the place we'd rather be. Metras offers us a meditation on 'The Economics of Rain' from war-ravaged Sarajevo where cold rain creates 'One cold more the world expectorates' and a mother '… hums to barter with night.'

Returning to Vienna, we watch the deaf and increasingly decrepit hulk of Beethoven navigate rainy streets, his iconic profile in that hat that could not 'corral that large head and surf of hair about to crash.' Unlike the poems of Assisi and Florence where we are told what we are likely to already know about St. Francis and Michelangelo, Metras gives us Beethoven and Vienna as mirrors of one another in a dark winter rain. And as we make our way west again, we see "A Full Moon In Switzerland" "I wonder" the speaker muses "how deep into the deep lake/ the moon's light knifes.." that last verb bringing the reader up short, in a good way.

We go on to find Oscar Wilde at his wife's grave, Wordsworth sleeping in Stone Henge, and a flight of fancy in which the English Channel has been drained and one can simply walk to France (though being cautious of sea birds "who may be so confused they drop/ at your feet no longer capable of flight." Metras summons the unexpected image and moment in these poems and offers them with music and momentum. "When I Saw The Wild Rabbit" is the most unexpected, rich juxtaposition of title and verse in the collection. We don't know from the title, where we'll be taken, and the short, intensely sensuous lyric drives the reader back to the title with a bit of an electric shock, to sort out the title's contribution. It's a pleasure to do that sorting.

A Review of *Jinx and Heavenly Calling* by Kelly DuMar (Lily Poetry Books)

Jackie Balter

In her second book length collection of poetry, *Jinx and Heavenly Calling*, Kelly DuMar poaches words and phrases from her own mother's love letters to her father and uses them to create a masterpiece of erasure poetry. Taking from letters written during her parent's courtship and the early weeks of their marriage DuMar creates a compelling collection which explores themes of love and commitment in an original and intimate way.

As DuMar explains in the "Notes on Form" section at the back of the book, each poem is taken from a single letter and the words and punctuation appear in the same order as in the source material. The visual background of each poem consists of images of the original letter or envelope, giving a partial glimpse into the original context and making clear the connection between the source material and DuMar's poems. The effect is at first jarring as it is unclear whether the poem is meant to include the original writing that appears or not, but as the reader delves further into the poems it becomes clear that that they can be read both ways, giving multiple meanings to poems depending on how the reader chooses to view them.

The book is split into four sections titled "Under a spell", "go a blizzard", "sneak a better anywhere", and "Gamble" each of which represents a different phase in a relationship. Starting with "Under a spell" DuMar explores the passion and turbulence of a new relationship. Poems such as "in a bad way" and "dress rehearsal" investigate the joy and fear that comes with falling in love. From the anxiety of "sticking neck out / heart tricked" ("in a bad way") to the joy of "week-ends / worth the head cold" ("dress rehearsal") the ups and downs of an early relationship are clearly displayed.

The next section, "go a blizzard", examines the next phase in a relationship in which there is more confidence in the partnership. Now engaged, gone are the anxieties of the early relationship, the fear that the other does not feel the same way or that they will leave. Now there is trust, as seen in "spree" where it is okay to "come too early / be too much". The thought of the future is ever-present in this section with poems such as "to get married" visualizing a future that would come to pass.

Thoughts of the future continue in "sneak a better anywhere" as the revelation of a pregnancy brings the future into more concrete reality. There is excitement and fear evident in poems like "worry" and "ours" as the uncertainties of the future expand to include a child.

The final section of the book "Gamble" is the shortest section but perhaps the most poignant as it explores the intimacies and intricacies of new marriage. In poems such as "husband" the marvel of being a newlywed is "hard to get / used to" making clear the transition that comes with becoming husband and wife.

As a whole, DuMar's *Jinx and Heavenly Calling* is a masterfully crafted exploration of the joys and difficulties of love and marriage. It is visually appealing and the images and words together evoke a sense of intimacy, making the reader feel as though they are intruding on private thoughts and in doing so delving deeper into the relationship on display than an outsider is typically allowed.

Biographies

Author

RUCHI ACHARYA, is the Founder and CEO of Wingless Dreamer Publisher, a global platform dedicated to uplifting writers and artists. Holding a summer graduation in English Literature from the University of Oxford, Ruchi's poetic prowess shines through her acclaimed work, including the poetry book "Off the Cliff".

JACKIE BALTER is a senior working towards her bachelor's degree in English at Lesley University. In addition to her studies she works as an intern at Nixes Mate and enjoys creative pursuits such as photography, painting, and crafting. Originally from Wayland, she currently lives in Arlington with her dog Sitka.

RUSTY BARNES is a poet and editor living in Revere MA with his family, and yes, many cats. His work appears widely online. Most recently, he published *HALF CRIME*, a story collection from Redneck Press.

RACHEL BECKER'S poetry has appeared or is forthcoming in journals including *Barely South Review*, *The Portland Review*, *The Rappahannock Review*, *The Shore*, *Maudlin House*, *The Tusculum Review*, and *RHINO*. She is also an assistant poetry editor for Porcupine Literary: A journal by and for teachers. She lives in Boston.

LAURIN BECKER MACIOS' books include the forthcoming YA verse novel *Calling Me Home* (Holiday House, 2026) and the poetry collection *Somewhere to Go*, winner of the 19th annual poetry award from Elixir Press. More of her work can be found at laurinbeckermacios.com.

LAUREL BENJAMIN is a Cider Press Review Book Award finalist. She has work forthcoming or published in *Lily Poetry Review, Nixes Mate, Pirene's Fountain, Cider Press Review, Taos Journal of Poetry*. She is affiliated with the Bay Area Women's Poetry Salon and reads for *Common Ground Review*.

A lifelong New Englander, **JEFF BERNSTEIN** would most have liked to have been, like Thoreau, "an inspector of snow-storms and rain-storms… [a] surveyor, if not of highways, then of forest paths and all across-lot routes." His new poetry collection, *The Ancient Ways*, was just published by Aldrich Press.

BETH BOYLAN lives and teaches high-school English near the ocean in New Jersey. Her poetry has been nominated for a Pushcart Prize and Best of the Net and appears in journals including *Rust + Moth, New York Quarterly, Glass: A Journal of Poetry, Whale Road Review*, and *Peatsmoke*. Beth's chapbook, *Third Rail*, is forthcoming from Kelsay Books.

ERIC BRAUDE grew up in South Africa. He won the 27th annual Eagle-Tribune/Robert Frost Foundation Spring Poetry Contest and wrote the front matter poem for the Grey Court Poets' anthology *Songs from the Castle's Remains*, published in 2013. Braude has published in *Poetica, South Florida Poetry Journal, Apple Valley Review, Constellations, I-70 Review*, and *J Journal*.

ROBERT CARR is the author of three collections: Amaranth (Indolent Books); The Unbuttoned Eye and The Heavy of Human Clouds (3: A Taos Press). Forthcoming collections include *Phallus Sprouting Leaves*, winner of the 2024 Rane Arroyo Chapbook Series, Seven Kitchens Press; and *Blue Memento*, Lily Poetry Books. robertcarr.org

JACQUELINE COLEMAN-FRIED is a poet living in Tuckahoe, NY. Her work has appeared in *New Verse News, Witcraft, Consequence, The Orchards Poetry Journal, pacificREVIEW*, and soon, *Streetlight Magazine*.

DALE COTTINGHAM has published in *Prairie Schooner, Ashville Poetry Review, Rain Taxi* and many others. He is the winner of the 2019 New

Millennium Award for Poem of the Year and was a finalist in the 2022 Great Midwest Poetry Contest. His debut volume of poems *Midwest Hymns,* was a finalist in the 2023 Best Book Awards for Poetry. He lives in Edmond, Oklahoma.

MARK DECARTERET has published in *The American Poetry Review, Asheville Poetry Review, BlazeVOX, Gargoyle, Hole in the Head* (which chose him as a finalist for Charles Simic Poetry Prize...), *Map Literary, New American Writing, On the Seawall, Posit,* and Nixes Mate (publisher of *For Lack of a Calling* and *lesser case*).

ROBIN DELLABOUGH'S debut collection, *Double Helix* (2022), includes a Pushcart Prize-nominated poem. Recent poems have appeared or are forthcoming in *Gyroscope, Nixes Mate, Yellow Arrow, Stoneboat, Halfway Down the Stairs, Mom Egg Review, Blue Unicorn, Negative Capability,* and other publications and anthologies.

JOHN DORSEY is the former Poet Laureate of Belle, MO. He is the author of several collections of poetry, including *Which Way to the River: Selected Poems: 2016-2020* (OAC Books, 2020), *Sundown at the Redneck Carnival,* (Spartan Press, 2022, and *Pocatello Wildflower,* (Crisis Chronicles Press, 2023). He may be reached at archerevans@yahoo.com.

SARA EDDY'S collection of poems, *Ordinary Fissures,* was released in May 2024 by Kelsay Books. She is also author of two chapbooks – *Tell the Bees* (A3 Press) and *Full Mouth* (Finishing Line), and has published widely in literary journals, including *Threepenny Review, Baltimore Review, Raleigh Review,* and *SWWIM,* among other venues.

CATHERINE FAHEY is a poet and librarian from Salem, Mass. When she's not reading and writing, she's knitting or dancing. Her chapbook *The Roses that Bloom at the End of the World* is available from Boston Accent Lit. You can read more of her work at magpiepoems.com.

SANDRA FEES lives in southeastern Pennsylvania where she is a Unitarian Universalist minister and past poet laureate of Berks County, PA. Her poems have been published in *Crab Creek Review, Whale Road Review, Witness,* and elsewhere.

CAL FREEMAN (he/him) is the author of the books *Fight Songs* and *Poolside at the Dearborn Inn*. His writing has appeared in *North American Review, Panoply, Oxford American, Atticus Review, Witness Magazine, Third Coast, Passages North* and elsewhere. His chapbook, *Yelping the Tegmine*, has just been released.

CHARLOTTE FRIEDMAN is a poet, author, translator and teacher. Her work has been published, most recently, in journals such as *The Timberline Review, Cagibi, Naugatuck River Review* and *Stonecoast Review*. Her translations of Ch'ol poetry (with Carol Rose Little) have appeared in World Literature Today, Arkansas International and elsewhere.

ED GAUDET is a writer and software entrepreneur who lives in Hanover, Massachusetts. His work has appeared in *Blood & Bourbon, Burningword Literary Journal, The Inflectionist Review, Panoply, Clade Song, Naugatuck River Review, Massachusetts Bards Poetry Review 2024,* and *Book of Matches, Lit.*

JACK GIAOUR (he/him/his) won the 2023/2024 BOOM Chapbook Contest from Bateau Press with his manuscript *hunting the bugs*. His work has appeared or is forthcoming in Fourteen Hills, Albatross Magazine, and the *Sonora Review*, among other journals. He sunlights as software manager for a steel fabricator just north of Boston.

ADAM GRABOWSKI is the author of the chapbook *Go on Bewilderment* (Attack Bear Press, 2020) and his poetry has appeared in such journals as *New Ohio Review, Sixth Finch, Ninth Letter*, and elsewhere. He currently lives in Western Massachusetts where he is the associate poetry editor for *The Maine Review*.

ELLY GUZIKOWSKI is a poet and recent graduate from Lesley University. His work is exploratory and nostalgic. Often touching on physical and personal development, he begs questions of the body and his place in the anthropocene. He is published in Mass poetry's 2024 undergrad anthology and a few local publications.

MATTHEW E. HENRY (MEH) is an educator, prose dabbler, and the author of six poetry collections. He is editor-in-chief of *The Weight*

Journal and an associate poetry editor at Rise Up Review. MEH can be found at MEHPoeting.com writing about education, race, religion, and burning oppressive systems to the ground.

KARINA JUTZI writes plays, poems, essays, screenplays and fiction. Her plays have been produced widely across the United States, and have been named among the Best of Equity Theater. Her poetry, essays, and comedy writing have been featured in various literary magazines both on and offline.

STEPHEN KAMPA is the author of four collections of poetry: *World Too Loud to Hear*, *Articulate as Rain*, *Bachelor Pad*, and *Cracks in the Invisible*. He teaches at Flagler College in St. Augustine, FL.

HANNAH LARRABEE'S *Wonder Tissue* won the Airlie Press Prize, and her recent chapbook – *The Observable Universe* – was longlisted for a Massachusetts Book Award. She lives in Salem, Massachusetts. hannahlarrabee.com

TOM LAUGHLIN is Coordinator of the Creative Writing Program at Middlesex Community College in Massachusetts. His poetry has appeared in *Green Mountains Review*, *Ibbetson Street*, *Drunk Monkeys*, *Main Street Rag*, and elsewhere. His chapbook, *The Rest of the Way*, was published by Finishing Line Press in 2022. More at TomLaughlinPoet.com

SARA LETOURNEAU is a poet, writing coach, editor, and open mic cohost from Massachusetts. Her debut poetry collection, *Wild Gardens*, is out now via Kelsay Books. Other recent and forthcoming work can be found in *Amethyst Review*, *Gyroscope Review*, *Remington Review*, and *Silver Birch Press*. Visit Sara online at heartofthestoryeditorial.com.

Bangladeshi writer **HUMAYUN MALIK'S** writings are published in local and international magazines. He has 25 published books. He was a journalist, government officer, and university teacher, now an advocate. Awards: Fair and Lovely, Daily News Paper Literary Award, Fiction Writer's Center Award.

JENNIFER MARTELLI has received fellowships from The Virginia Center for the Creative Arts and the Massachusetts Cultural Council. Her work has appeared in The Academy of American Poets Poem-A-Day, *Poetry*, and elsewhere. jennmartelli.com

GRACE MASSEY is a poet, dancer, and socializer of feral cats. She lives in Massachusetts with her husband, Michael, and a formerly feral cat. Grace has degrees in English from Smith College and Boston University. Her poems have been published in numerous journals, including *Quartet*, *Thimble*, *RockPaperPoem*, and *One Art*.

JOAN MAZZA worked as a microbiologist, psychotherapist, and taught workshops on dreams and nightmares. She is the author of six psychology books, including *Dreaming Your Real Self*. Her poetry has appeared in *Atlanta Review*, *The Comstock Review*, *Prairie Schooner*, *Slant*, *Poet Lore*, and *The Nation*. She lives in rural Virginia.

CLARE MCMILLAN earned a Ph.D. in German Studies from Cornell. She began writing fiction and poetry during the dark days of the pandemic and has had work published in *Failbetter* and *Wintermute*. She is currently completing a novel. She lives in Ithaca, New York.

BRIAN MOSHER is a writer whose work has appeared or will appear soon in *Rituals* (from Anomaly Poetry), *Coneflower Cafe*, *Written Tales*, *Oddball Magazine*, *eMerge*, *Alien Buddha Zine*, *Esoterica Magazine*, *Half and One Magazine*, and *Verse Wrights*.

MIRIAM O'NEAL'S newest collection is *The Half-Said Things* (Nixes Mate, 2022). She is Poet Laureate of Plymouth, MA. She has published in *The Waxed Lemon*, *North Dakota Quarterly*, and elsewhere. New work will appear in *Lily Poetry Review* soon. She hosts Poetry the Art of Words in Plymouth, MA.

KAREN POPPY (she/her; non-binary) has work published in numerous literary journals, magazines, and anthologies. Her debut poetry collection, *Diving At The Lip Of The Water*, is published by Beltway Editions (2023). An attorney licensed in California and Texas, Karen Poppy lives in the San Francisco Bay Area. More at karenpoppy.com.

MICHAEL QUATTRONE (he/him) is the author of *Rhinoceroses* (2006 New School Chapbook Award). His work is included in the Best *American Erotic Poems* (Scribner, 2008) and the *Incredible Sestina Anthology* (Write Bloody, 2013). Recent poems appear in *Bennington Review, Salamander,* and *Poet Lore*.

SUSANNA RICH – poet, Emmy Award nominee, Fulbright Fellow, and Founding Producer of Wild Nights Productions, LLC – tours her musical Shakespeare's *itches: The Women v. Will and one-woman performances of her five books, most recently *Beware the House* and *SHOUT! Poetry for Suffrage.* Visit at wildnightsproductions.com.

BRAD ROSE was born and raised in Los Angeles and lives in Boston. He is the author of six collections of poetry and flash fiction: *WordInEdgeWise, Lucky Animals, No. Wait. I Can Explain., Pink X-Ray, de/tonations,* and *Momentary Turbulence*. His website is bradrosepoetry.com

BUFFY SHUTT writes poetry and short fiction. She is a two-time Pushcart and Best of the Net nominee. Her work appears in many journals. Her poetry collection, *Recruit to Deny* will be published in 2024. Her chapbooks, *Memos from the 20th 21st Century,* and *animal magnetism* are out now.

ZVI A. SESLING, Brookline, MA Poet Laureate 2017-2020, edits *Muddy River Poetry Review* and *10X10 Flash Fiction Stories*. He authored seven poetry books and two flash fiction books, *Secret Behind The Gate,* and *Wheels*. A joint collection with Paul Beckman *40 Stories* will be published in 2024.

NEIL SILBERBLATT is the founder/director of Voices of Poetry. His poems have appeared in numerous literary journals, including *River Heron Review, Plume Poetry Journal, Mom Egg Review, Lily Poetry Review, Tiferet Journal, American Journal of Poetry,* and *Tikkun Daily*. Silberblatt's poetry collections are *So Far, So Good, Present Tense,* and *Past Imperfect*.

RUTH SMULLIN lives in greater Boston. Her poetry has been published in *Atlanta Review, Ibbetson Street, Main Street Rag, Naugatuck River Review,*

Sow's Ear Poetry Review, and The Aurorean among others. Her chapbook, The Open Door, was published by Finishing Line Press in 2020.

SUSAN ISLA TEPPER is the author of 12 published books of fiction and poetry, and five Stage Plays. Her newest book is a novel titled Hair of a Fallen Angel soon to be released by Spuyten Duyvil Press. susantepper.com

MARK WALSH is an English professor at Massasoit Community College in Brockton, MA. His Chapbook In The Garden of Fortune, was published by Lily Poetry Review Books in May of 2024. Recent poetry publications include Beatnick Cowboy, Abandoned Mine, Rituals and Choeofpleirn Press.

JON WESICK is a regional editor of the San Diego Poetry Annual. He's published hundreds of poems and stories in small-press journals. His most recent books are The Shaman in the Library, and The Prague Deception. jonwesick.com

GERALD YELLE'S books include The Holyoke Diaries, Mark My Word and the New World Order, and Dreaming Alone and with Others. His chapbooks include No Place I Would Rather Be, and A Box of Rooms. He lives in Amherst, Massachusetts and is a member of the Florence Poets Society.

Colophon

The text is set in Maiola, a contemporary typeface inspired by early Czech type design. The titles are set in Tablet Gothic, a grotesque sans-serif grounded in 19th century British typography. Both fonts were designed by Veronika Burian, a type designer and co-founder of the independent type foundry TypeTogether. She is also involved with Alphabettes.org, a showcase of work and research on lettering, typography, and type design by women.

RECENT TITLES FROM NIXES MATE

Spirit Spout · Devon Balwit

Dot Girl · Linda Carney-Goodrich

Wild Pack of the Living · Eileen Cleary

lesser case · Mark Decarteret

Series · Mari Deweese

Now Calls Me Daughter · Christine Jones

Feast of the Seven Fishes · Linda Lamenza

Album of Not · Eve F. W. Linn

The Half-Said Things · Miriam O'Neal

Unfoldings · Clara Eugenia Ronderos

Banana Bread · J. D. Scimgeour

Nike Adjusting Her Sandal · Anastasia Vassos

It's Not Love Till Someone Loses an Eye · Clay Ventre

Thieves' Canto · Marc Vincenz

SUBSCRIBE TO NIXES MATE REVIEW.

Get 2 issues per year for $25.
Go to nixesmate.pub/subscribe

BECOME A PATRON OF NIXES MATE.

For $50 receive two issues of *Nixes Mate Review*, plus our latest book, and a special literary treat.

For $100 receive two issues of *Nixes Mate Review*, plus our latest three books, and a special literary treat.

For $250 receive two issues of *Nixes Mate Review*, plus our latest three books, and all the available limited edition broadsides.

For $500 receive two issues of *Nixes Mate Review*, plus all the books in our catalog.

For $1000 receive all current and future issues of *Nixes Mate Review*, plus all the books in our catalog, all the available limited edition broadsides and chapbooks, various special literary treats, and all our future books.

42° 19' 47.9" N · 70° 56' 43.9" W

Nixes Mate is a navigational hazard in Boston Harbor used during the colonial period to gibbet and hang pirates and mutineers.

Nixes Mate Books features small-batch artisanal literature, created by writers who use all 26 letters of the alphabet and then some, honing their craft the time-honored way: one line at a time.

nixesmate.pub

www.ingramcontent.com/pod-product-compliance
Lightning Source LLC
Chambersburg PA
CBHW081432070526
44586CB00020B/2557